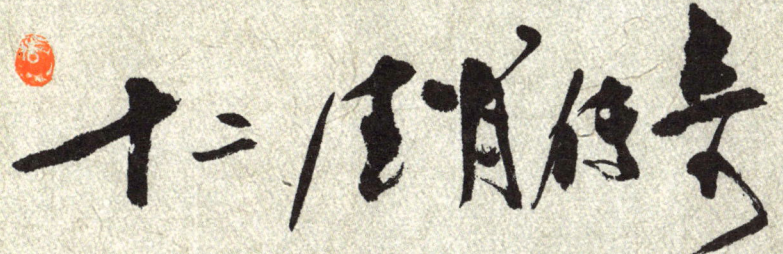

Legends of Chinese Zodiac

（中英文版）

韦 诚 李益芳 编著
李 雪 左娟霞   译

北京师范大学出版集团
安徽大学出版社

图书在版编目(CIP)数据

十二生肖传奇:汉、英/韦诚,李益芳编著.—合肥:安徽大学出版社,2019.4
 ISBN 978-7-5664-1804-3

Ⅰ.①十… Ⅱ.①韦…②李… Ⅲ.①十二生肖—通俗读物—汉、英 Ⅳ.①K892.21-49

中国版本图书馆 CIP 数据核字(2019)第 050147 号

十二生肖传奇(中英文版)	韦 诚 李益芳 编著

出版发行：北京师范大学出版集团
　　　　　安 徽 大 学 出 版 社
　　　　　(安徽省合肥市肥西路 3 号 邮编 230039)
　　　　　www.bnupg.com.cn
　　　　　www.ahupress.com.cn
印　　刷：合肥鸿祈印务有限公司
经　　销：全国新华书店
开　　本：148mm×210mm
印　　张：3.625
字　　数：91 千字
版　　次：2019 年 4 月第 1 版
印　　次：2019 年 4 月第 1 次印刷
定　　价：28.00 元
ISBN 978-7-5664-1804-3

策划编辑：李　梅　李　雪　　　　装帧设计：李　军
责任编辑：李　雪　　　　　　　　美术编辑：李　军
责任印制：赵明炎

版权所有　侵权必究
反盗版、侵权举报电话：0551-65106311
外埠邮购电话：0551-65107716
本书如有印装质量问题,请与印制管理部联系调换。
印制管理部电话：0551-65106311

前言

十二生肖作为一种贯穿中国历史的文化符号,诉说着一个民族的图腾情节,演绎着一个东方大国的生活方式,也寄托着一代代炎黄子孙的精神理想。它作为中华民族智慧的结晶,已经渗透到十几亿人的生命与信仰之中,是"龙的传人"永不褪色的独特烙印。

文化是一个国家、一个民族的灵魂。生肖文化是中国传统文化的重要组成部分。习近平总书记提出:"推动中华优秀传统文化创造性转化、创新性发展……"弘扬中华优秀传统文化是我们义不容辞的责任。

我们对十二生肖文化的兴趣源于对动物世界的好奇和热爱。继 2017 年《走近动物系列》(中英文版)出版后,我们努力追寻生肖文化的源头,结合神话故事和动物传奇故事,以挖掘和阐发传统文化真善美为主旨进行创作。在地方文化学者王永泉先生、科普文学艺术界专家和社会各界的支

持和鼓励下,《十二生肖传奇》(中英文版)终于问世了。

  书中妙趣横生的故事、生动鲜活的图片,体现了东方文化特有的瑰丽奇观。希望这本书在给读者,尤其是青少年读者提供传统文化知识之外,还能激起其热爱传统文化、热爱中华民族之情。同时,我们也希望读者努力汲取生肖文化的精华,弘扬中华优秀传统文化向上、向善的精神,使其跨越时空、跨越国度,生生不息!

编著者:

Foreword

Chinese zodiac, also known as *shengxiao*, is an important cultural symbol throughout the Chinese history. The zodiac signs reflect the cultural totems and lifestyle of an oriental nation, and endow the ideology of Chinese descendants, generation after generation. The zodiac culture is sowed deeply into our lives and beliefs, being not only the crystallization of the wisdom of Chinese people, but also a sear to "the Descendants of the Dragon".

Culture is the soul of a nation. In China, Zodiac culture is an important part of it. President Xi Jinping said, "We must improve the creative transformation and development of prominent traditional Chinese culture." It is our responsibility to pass on the culture.

Our interest in the Chinese zodiac culture originated in our curiosity and love to the animal world. After the publication of *Approaching the Animals Series*, we traced the origin of

十二生肖传奇（中英文版）

culture, combined the legends to the vivid stories happened all over the world, and created our new work with the goal "to excavate and encourage the true, the good and the beautiful of the traditional culture". With the encouragement and support of the local cultural scholar Mr. Wang Yongquan and other experts in educational literature and arts, this book finally meets its readers.

The interesting stories and vivid pictures demonstrate the unique and splendid cultural highlights from an eastern nation. We wish that our readers, especially the youth, through reading the booklet, will gain not only the knowledge about the traditional culture, but also affection for our culture and nation. At the same time, we wish them to take in the essence of zodiac culture, hold on to the spirit of enterprise and kindness within our splendid culture, and pass it on to the future generations, other counties, and to keep it alive forever.

Compilers: Wei Cheng & Li Yifang

Contents

第一部分　十二生肖文化漫谈 / 1
Part One　About the Culture of Chinese Zodiac

十二生肖的起源 / 6
Origin of Chinese Zodiac / 10

十二生肖的基本内涵 / 17
The Cultural Connotation of Chinese Zodiac / 19

十二生肖与民间习俗 / 22
Folk Traditions about Chinese Zodiac / 26

十二生肖传奇（中英文版）

第二部分　十二生肖的传奇 / 37
Part Two　The Legends of Twelve Zodiac Animals

鼠的传奇 / 38
The Legend of Rat / 40

牛的传奇 / 43
The Legend of Ox / 45

虎的传奇 / 48
The Legend of Tiger / 50

兔的传奇 / 54
The Legend of Rabbit / 56

龙的传奇 / 60
The Legend of Dragon / 62

蛇的传奇 / 66
The Legend of Snake / 68

目录

马的传奇 / 71
The Legend of Horse / 73

羊的传奇 / 76
The Legend of Goat / 78

猴的传奇 / 81
The Legend of Monkey / 83

鸡的传奇 / 87
The Legend of Rooster / 89

狗的传奇 / 93
The Legend of Dog / 96

猪的传奇 / 100
The Legend of Pig / 102

第一部分
十二生肖文化漫谈

Part One
About the Culture of Chinese Zodiac

十二生肖传奇（中英文版）

中华传统文化源远流长，生肖文化作为其中的一部分，与炎黄子孙的生命观、自然观、宗教观和哲学理念密切相关。十二生肖是鼠、牛、虎、兔、龙、蛇、马、羊、猴、鸡、狗、猪这十二种动物。

关于十二生肖的由来，据文献记载，在古代中原地区，自帝舜时代开始，人们就使用十天干和十二地支相配合的"干支纪年法"。"十二生肖"的说法最早见于世界上第一部诗歌总集《诗经》。《诗经·小雅·车攻》："吉日庚午，既差我马。"又见于《礼记·月令·季冬》："出土牛，以送寒气。"据湖北云

十二生肖文化漫谈

梦睡虎地和甘肃天水放马滩20世纪70年代中期出土的秦简可知,先秦时期,比较完整的生肖系统已经存在。与现代相同的十二生肖最早记载于东汉王充的《论衡》卷三《物势篇》;清代梁章钜在《浪迹丛谈·续谈》中也转述了《论衡》的记载。

十二生肖是十二地支的形象化代表,即子(鼠)、丑(牛)、寅(虎)、卯(兔)、辰(龙)、巳(蛇)、午(马)、未(羊)、申(猴)、酉(鸡)、戌(狗)和亥(猪)。随着人类社会的发展,十二生肖逐渐与民间习俗与宗教信仰相融合,表现在婚姻、事业、年运等方面,每一种生肖都有丰富的传说。

Traditional Chinese culture has a long history. Being a part of it, the zodiac culture has a close relationship with Chinese people's concept of life, nature, religion and philosophy. The twelve Chinese zodiac signs, are Rat, Ox, Tiger, Rabbit, Dragon, Snake, Horse, Goat, Monkey, Rooster, Dog, and Pig.

Its origin is, according to the literature, the method of

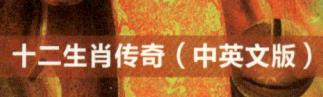
十二生肖传奇（中英文版）

measuring years based on the Ten Heavenly Stems and Twelve Earthly Branches, dating from the Period of the Emperor Shun in central China. "Chinese zodiac" originated in *The Book of Songs*, the oldest collection of poems in the world. Chapter Xiaoya, Chegong of *The Book of Songs* recorded, "In a blessed day of Gengwu, I travel with some well-chosen horses." In *The Book of Rites*, Chapter Yueling, Jidong, "people make clay ox to drive away the coldness." Some bamboo slips of Qin Dynasty were unearthed in Shuihu Area of Yunmeng County of Hubei Province and Fangma Beach of Tianshui City of Gansu Province, in the middle of the 1970s. They showed that in the early Qin Dynasty, a relatively complete zodiac system was already formed. The record of Chinese zodiac same with nowadays dated to *Lun Heng*, by Wang Chong of East Han Dynasty, Chapter Three, the chapter about the state of things. Liang Zhanggang of Qing Dynasty also quoted the words in *Lun Heng* about Chinese zodiac in his work *Langji Congtan: Xutan*.

　　The twelve Chinese zodiac animals represent the Twelve Earthly Branches: Rat as *Zi*, Ox as *Chou*, Tiger as *Yin*, Rabbit as *Mao*, Dragon as *Chen*, Snake as *Si*, Horse as *Wu*, Goat as

Wei, Monkey as *Shen*, Rooster as *You*, Dog as *Xu*, and Pig as *Hai*. With the development of society, the Chinese zodiac signs are merging with the folk beliefs, and each zodiac sign has rich stories and legends. Chinese zodiac provided people's lives with new cultural elements, as in marriage, career, luck of the year, etc.

十二生肖传奇（中英文版）

十二生肖的起源

关于十二生肖的起源，众说纷纭，比较有代表性的说法有以下三种。

1. **图腾说** 原始社会的先民常用某种动物或自然现象的象征图形作为本氏族的保护神和标志，即图腾。《山海经》中人和野兽的混合形象就是远古各地的图腾神。夏族的图腾是熊或鱼，商族的图腾是玄鸟，周族的图腾则有龙、鸟、龟、

十二生肖文化漫谈

犬、虎诸说。十二生肖除龙为虚幻之物，其余皆日常可见。其可分两类，即"六畜"（马、牛、羊、鸡、狗和猪）和"六兽"（鼠、虎、兔、龙、蛇和猴），前者是人们为了经济目的而驯养的，后者则是在一定程度上骚扰人类生活，令先民心生畏惧的动物。因此，这些动物被作为本氏族的名号标记来崇拜。

2. 岁星说　　木星十二年运行一周天，从木星位置可确定年度。清朝马国翰的《玉函山房辑佚书》认为，每十二年，"三岁穰，三岁毁，三岁康，三岁旱"。植物兴衰和动物生活环境存在周期，草食动物和肉食、杂食动物在不同年份的生活条件大不相同。古人认为，动物兴衰与木星年有关，将不同年份出生的人比喻为当年生长旺盛的动物，从而形成生肖动物。

3. 取数说　　生肖取数十二，暗合古人对自然现象的归纳性认识。中国先民感受到寒暑交替、植物枯荣的周期，以之为"一岁"。月亮的盈亏周期也与"岁"息息相关，十二次月圆正好一岁。《周礼·春官·冯相氏》："掌十有二岁、十有二月、十有二辰。""十二"这个数字除了计量年和月以外，还用来计量时辰。这个数字在其他方面也有很多应用。《左传·哀公七年》："周之王也，制礼，上物不过十二。以为天之大数也。"《国语·晋语四》："黄帝之子二十五宗，其得姓者十四人,为十二姓。"《后汉书·苟爽传》:"故天子娶十二妇,天之数也。诸侯以下各有等差,事之降也。"古人还把"十二天象"作为古代对天气的统称,即暗、阴、雨、雪、冰、雾、露、霜、风、沙、雷和电。另外,"十二经脉"是中医对人体经络的认知;古代音乐有"十二律";饮食有"十二食";穿衣有"十二衣",等等。

关于十二生肖的起源,除了以上三说,还有五行阴阳说、星宿说和外来说等多种说法,而最为人们喜闻乐见的还是玉皇大帝通过比赛给动物排名的神话故事。

据传,在很久以前,人们不会计算自己的年龄,就去请教玉皇大帝。玉帝决定选择十二只动物来代表当年出生的人的属相,以记录人们的岁数。于是召集所有的动物,要举办一场过河比赛,规定最先游过河到达天宫的十二只动物胜出。

比赛开始后,老鼠央求憨厚老实、善于游泳的牛背它过河。眼看终点已在眼前,它狡猾地向前一跃冲线,竟夺得冠军。牛只得屈居第二位。老虎紧随其后,获得第三名。兔子一蹦一跳地踩着其他动物的背,冲到前面得了第四名。可是由于太紧张,摔倒在河岸的一块大石头上,将嘴磕成了三瓣。龙和蛇本来是游泳高手,但龙忙于为人类降雨,等它得到消息赶回来参加比赛,因耽误了时间,所以只得了第五名。蛇自以为游泳本领高,就大意轻敌,反而落在了龙后面,得了第六名。马、羊和猴分别占据第七至九名。鸡和狗找了一段树干,一起站在上面过河。传说鸡原本是四只脚,两只脚在过河时卡在树干的缝里折断了,后来只剩下两只了。它只拿了第十名。狗站在树干上,只顾着观看其他动物的比赛而忘了自己也在参赛的事,名次排在鸡的后面。眼看太阳快落山了,猪挺着圆鼓鼓的肚子,不慌不忙地过了河,占据了最后一席。

于是,十二年为一轮、每一年由一种动物代表的年龄计算方法就这样定下来了,古人也就自此有了计算年龄的方法。

人们提出疑问:为什么猫没有参赛?原来,当时老鼠和猫是好朋友,猫经常睡懒觉,就请求老鼠比赛当天叫它起床。老鼠却没有叫醒它,独自去参赛了。等猫起床匆匆渡过河赶到天宫的时候,却发现一切都晚了,前十二名的动物们正在开庆功宴。从此,老鼠虽然凭借小聪明赢得了冠军,却和猫成了冤家对头。

十二生肖传奇（中英文版）

Origin of Chinese Zodiac

There are a variety of sayings about the origin of the twelve Chinese zodiac signs, the following are three representative ones.

1. From Totem The ancestors of primitive society used signs of an animal or a phenomenon to represent the protecting god of their clans, i.e., totems. *The Classic of Mountains and Seas* recorded many totem gods from different places in ancient times, which were combined images of men and beasts.

十二生肖文化漫谈

Totems of the Xia Clan were bear or fish; of the Shang Clan, Fenice; of the Zhou clan, dragon, bird, turtle, dog, or tiger according to different literatures. All animals in Chinese zodiac, except the illusory dragon were close to people's daily lives. They could be divided into two groups: six livestock (horse, ox, goat, rooster, dog, pig) and six beasts (rat, tiger, rabbit, dragon, snake, monkey), the former being raised by people for economic reasons, and the later that to a certain degree harass people or put fear into their hearts. Therefore these animals were worshiped as signs of certain clans.

2. From the movement of Jupiter Jupiter revolves around the sun in a circle of twelve years. Our ancestors defined the years by its position in the sky. Ma Guohan in Qing Dynasty, said in his *Addendum Book of the House on Yuhan Mountain*, that every twelve years had "three years of harvest, three years of poor crops, three years of good growing, and three years of drought". Periods occurred in the rise and decline of plants and animals. Herbivores, predators and omnivores had varied living conditions in different years. Ancient people thought that the rise and decline of animals were related to the years marked by

Jupiter. They referred the people who were born in a particular year to the animals that thrived in that year. In this way, the zodiac animals came into shape.

3. From counting The number "twelve" of Chinese zodiac correlated with people's conclusive understanding of natural phenomena. Our ancestors found the circle of the change of climate and the growth of plants, so they defined the circle as "a year". The waxing and waning of moon also went with the circle, thus twelve waxings amounted to a year in time. Chapter "Offices of Spring, Fengxiangshi" *in The Rites of Zhou* recorded, "Twelve years form a circle, and so do twelve months and twelve two-hour periods." The number "twelve" also marked hours, other than years and months. It was also applied in many other fields. *The Spring and Autumn Annals*, Chapter for Duke Ai of Lu, recorded, "In the Zhou Dynasty, people created the rites of Zhou, adopting a strict hierarchical system for social rites such as clothing and rituals. *The Rites of Zhou* stipulated that the highest rank is marked by the number twelve." *History of the Spring and Autumn Nations* (*Guoyu*), Jin's Chapter, recorded, "Among the twenty-five sons of the

Yellow Emperor, fourteen of them were granted a surname, and in all they had twelve surnames." *History of the later Han Dynasty*, Chapter of Xun Shuang, recorded, "Twelve is the highest number of heaven thus the emperor's brides should be not more than twelve in number. The number of the dukes' wives decreases according to their positions." Besides, the number twelve existed in all walks of life, for example "the twelve celestial phenomena" referred to all kinds of weathers: dark, cloudy, rainy, snowy, icy, foggy, dewy, frosty, windy, sandy, stormy, and lightening; Traditional Chinese medicine held that human body had twelve meridians and collaterals; ancient Chinese music had twelve tones; also we had "twelve diets" and "twelve clothing".

Besides, there are also other sayings that Chinese zodiac is from the Five Elements and yin-yang, constellation, or foreign nations. The most interesting one is about a contest held by the Jade Emperor to rank the animals.

It was said that thousands of years ago, people had no idea about how to count their ages. So they came to the Jade Emperor for help. The emperor decided to choose twelve

animals to represent the zodiac of the people who were born in each year, to count people's ages. He summoned all the animals, and held a river-crossing contest, bidding that the twelve animals that crossed the river first would be the winners.

During the contest, the rat begged the simple and honest ox which was good at swimming to carry it across the river. When the finishing line was close, it jumped ahead of the ox and became champion, to everyone's surprise. The ox had to be the second, followed by the tiger. The rabbit hopped on other

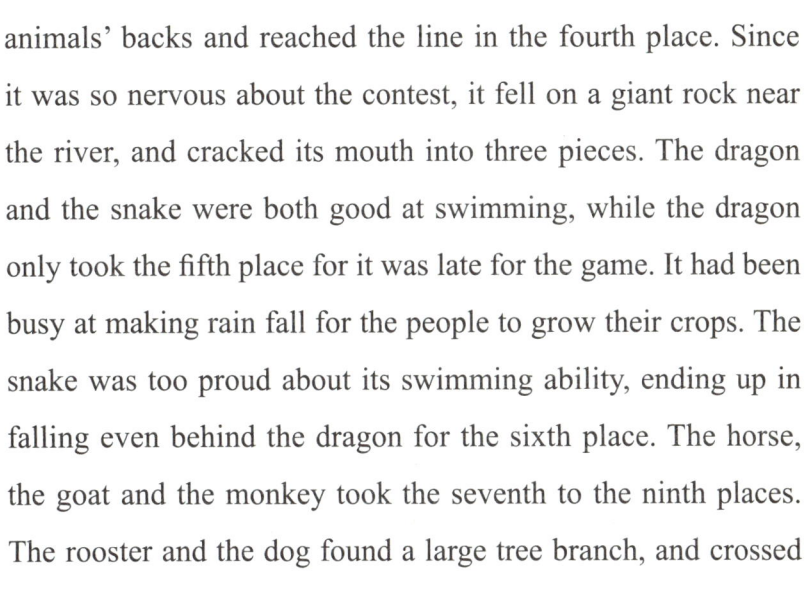

animals' backs and reached the line in the fourth place. Since it was so nervous about the contest, it fell on a giant rock near the river, and cracked its mouth into three pieces. The dragon and the snake were both good at swimming, while the dragon only took the fifth place for it was late for the game. It had been busy at making rain fall for the people to grow their crops. The snake was too proud about its swimming ability, ending up in falling even behind the dragon for the sixth place. The horse, the goat and the monkey took the seventh to the ninth places. The rooster and the dog found a large tree branch, and crossed the river standing on it. The rooster was said to have four legs in the past; it broke two for they were stuck in the tree branch. It got the tenth place. The dog was over-thrilled about watching other animals crossing the river and forgot about its own game, so it fell behind the rooster. At sunset, the pig peacefully crossed the river with its round belly, and took the last position.

Since then, people began to adopt an age counting method involving a twelve-year circle with each animal standing for one year.

You might ask: why wasn't the cat in the contest? It

appeared that it overslept and missed the contest. The cat was a good friend to the rat before the story happened. It asked the rat to wake it up for the contest, while the rat didn't. The cat woke up and hurried for the contest, only to find the twelve winners were holding a celebrating party. Although the rat won the contest, it turned its friend to a mortal enemy.

十二生肖文化漫谈

十二生肖的 基本内涵

　　十二生肖,又称"属相",其基本内涵是十二地支结合代表人出生年份的十二种动物,即子鼠、丑牛、寅虎、卯兔、辰龙、巳蛇、午马、未羊、申猴、酉鸡、戌狗、亥猪。十二生肖动物的习性被人们赋予诸多文化内涵,它们在中国人精神世界中,超越了普通动物的自然属性,达到了接受人们尊崇和膜拜的地步。只有将动物的自然属性与人文意义相融合,才能构成完整的生肖动物形象。

鼠的繁殖能力强,民间常将其作为生殖崇拜的象征。它们对灾祸有灵敏的感知,因此矿工将对它们的崇拜和禁忌代代传承。东北煤矿工人尊鼠为"鼠仙",忌讳捕鼠,在井下吃饭,还分出一些饭菜来喂老鼠。云南一个旧矿区还有座"耗子庙"。

虎是百兽之王,被人们认为是凶猛与阳刚的象征。与之对应的"寅"字在甲骨文中如箭矢状,《说文》中"寅"意为"阳气上升,虽上有冻土,必破土而出",与虎的特点相契合。

中国民间素有对龙的崇拜。《周易·乾卦》以龙虎比喻乾坤、天地,龙飞在天、虎行于地。"龙凤呈祥"图案是中华民族最有代表性的形象符号,在唐代后广为流传,象征着皇帝和皇后的权力,也象征夫妻的美满结合,还可象征精神与物质的阴阳两极调和。

《韩诗外传》概括鸡有"五德":"头戴冠者,文也;足搏距者,武也;敌在前敢斗者,勇也;见食相呼者,义也;守夜不失时者,信也。"故鸡有"德禽"的雅号。

人们在传说和现实中经常赞颂狗的忠诚。《述异记》载,西晋陆机的"黄耳",为主人送信,劳累而亡。《搜神记》中的黑龙犬,在火灾中,用水沾湿醉酒的主人使其幸存。

十二生肖文化漫谈

每个生肖都被人们赋予了不同的精神品质,使得这一中国特有的文化现象生生不息。

The Cultural Connotation of Chinese Zodiac

The twelve Chinese zodiac signs, also known as "*shuxiang*" in Chinese, are twelve animals representing people's year of birth associated with the Twelve Earthly Branches, including Rat, Ox, Tiger, Rabbit, Dragon, Snake, Horse, Goat, Monkey, Rooster, Dog, and Pig. The natural habits of the twelve Chinese zodiac animals are given many cultural connotations. They mean much more than what they are to the Chinese people, who worship and respect them. The images of these twelve animals are complete only when we combine their natural characters and symbolic meanings.

Rats are fertile, and they are a sign of the production worship. They also enjoy a keen sense to danger, so the mining

十二生肖传奇（中英文版）

workers respect them, and pass their worship and awe to them from generation to generation. Mining workers in the northeastern provinces revere them as "the fairy rats". They never trap the rats, and even give them food when dining under the mines. An old mining area in Yunnan Province has a temple for the rats.

Tiger is thought to be the king of all the beasts and a symbol of fierceness and masculinity. The *Yin* character, from the Twelve Earthly Branches representing the tiger, has the shape of an arrow. In *Explaining Characters*, *Yin* means "*Yangqi* moves from inside of the earth, breaking through even the frozen earth beneath it", matching with the power of tiger.

The worship to dragon is a tradition in China. *The Book of Changes* referred the sky and earth to the dragon and tiger, for the former flies in the sky and the later walks on the ground. The picture of "prosperity brought by a dragon and phoenix" was symbolic of Chinese culture after Tang Dynasty, meaning the power of the emperor and empress, the perfect combination of a couple, and the harmony between matters and spirits.

The Unauthorized Biography of Han Ying's Poems

summarized the "five merits" of the rooster: the comb as education; the claws as martial arts; the fighting spirit as bravery; calling each other when finding food as loyalty; punctuality in the morning crow as integrity. Therefore, the rooster is also named "the bird of merits".

People praise the loyalty of dogs very often. *Yishu Ji* recorded that the dog named "yellow-ear", owned by Lu Ji, a famous calligrapher in the Western Jin Dynasty, carried a letter for its master and died of tiredness. The "black dragon dog" in *Soushen Ji* saved its drunken master by splattering water on him in a fire.

Each zodiac sign is given some special characters by people, which helps this unique culture to pass on.

十二生肖传奇（中英文版）

十二生肖与民间习俗

　　以生肖动物为主题的民俗活动丰富多彩，其表现形式主要以岁时节令、社交礼仪、娱乐游艺、服饰饮食等方面为主。由于社会生活方式的变化、民族和地域的差异，这些活动在内容和形式上也会有所变化和改进。

　　清朝时，农历正月廿五为"填仓节"，粮商米贩祭"仓神"老鼠。据清代潘荣升的《帝京岁时纪胜》记载："当此新正节过，仓廪为虚，应复置而实之。"填仓节当晚不许点灯，为了当晚不影响老鼠嫁女。到了老鼠嫁女日，人们炒黄豆拌以红糖，撒于屋角。该日的习俗，各地并不统一。有的地区在屋角撒盐巴米粒，称"老鼠分钱"。有的地区制作"蒸瞎老鼠"，正月十四用面捏成十二只老鼠，不捏眼睛，用蒸笼蒸熟，待元宵节时摆上供桌，点灯烧香祈求老鼠勿伤庄稼。

　　在现代农村比较流行的鞭春牛，又称"打春"，意在劝民农耕，宣告新年劳作开始。村民在纸牛肚里装入五谷，鞭后散落，象征"五谷丰登，谷流满地"。清代每年给地方下发《春

十二生肖文化漫谈

牛芒神图》。图中春牛各部位颜色根据当年干支与五行阴阳的关系设计,芒神的年纪、服饰、姿态也是如此,起到历书的作用。

各地都可以看到布老虎玩具。人们认为,虎是孩子的保护神,孩子们戴虎头帽,穿虎头鞋,可以得到虎神的庇佑,健康成长。外甥生日舅舅送他们虎枕,也能当玩具。有些省份,外甥满月,舅舅会送黄布虎,进门时折断虎尾,寓意"丢掉坎坷"。一些少数民族孩子佩戴虎爪和虎牙以驱鬼辟邪。历史上,汉代盛行"画虎于门",以虎为门神来镇宅,这一习俗最早可追溯到周代。旧时,华北流行在正厅悬挂年画《镇宅神虎图》,上书:"神虎下高山,降魔到人间。善家买了去,四季保平安。"

我国关于龙的习俗更是源远流长。二月二"龙抬头",民间认为,蛰伏的龙抬起了头,雨水渐多。人们在这天理发,希望像龙那样精神。北方人家用彩纸、草秸穿成串悬于房梁,称"穿龙尾"。这天要吃面条、烙饼或水饺,分别象征龙须、龙鳞和龙耳。每月都有关于龙的节日,如正月的云南瑶族祭龙节,三月山东祭龙王,四月山西大同雷音寺会,五月浙江嘉兴的"分龙日",六月晒龙袍,七月的无锡龙娘庙会……

北方游牧民族特别崇拜马。保安族流传神话"雪白马神";达斡尔族称神马为"温古",该神马不准女人骑;满族也有供奉神马的习俗。

上古神话中名叫"獬豸"的独角神羊,是司法审判之神皋陶的助手。王充《论衡·是应》:"皋陶治狱,其罪疑者,令羊触之。有罪则触,无罪则不触。"

直到今天,在民间还流行"本命年"的说法。本命年指十二年一遇的农历属相所在的年份,俗称"属相年"。"本命年犯太岁,太岁当头坐,无喜必有祸",本命年被视为不吉之年,故又称"坎儿年"。各地都有本命年挂红避邪的习俗。大年三十,逢本命年,大人小孩都换上红内衣红内裤,扎红腰带,最好再佩戴红色饰物,如红丝绳、红项圈等,此所谓"本

命红"。一些地方，本命年除夕夜忌出门，已婚男子还要妇人陪伴。

古人重视取名，名字需要弥补运势不足，生肖是起名的重要参考。宋朝文人邹应龙，生于乾道八年壬辰（1172年），故取名"应龙"。相传唐伯虎生于寅年寅月寅日，故取名"唐寅"。过去民间流行给孩子取贱名为乳名，认为这样孩子好养活。于是属狗的作家老舍乳名叫"小狗尾巴"，属羊的画家叶浅予乳名是"阿羊"。

汉族凡重大祭祀必以猪作为祭品，并以猪头为重，俗称"猪头三牲"。吴谷人《新年杂咏》："杭俗，岁终祀神尚猪首……选皱纹如寿字者，谓之'寿字猪头'。"现今江浙一带在腊月仍储备腌制咸猪头为年货。清明节部分地区的居民爱用烤猪祭祖，俗语"太公分猪肉，人人有份"，指祭后全家分食祭品。过去在有些地方，凡家庭遭受病灾不幸，家中长者设香案打"母猪鬼"以驱邪，认为"杀死一母猪鬼，驱除一个邪"。祭时选黄道吉日，杀老母猪，将其内脏等摆在堂屋，祭完吃掉。人们的生活中，在婚姻、农事、性格和国运等方面，还有诸多与生肖信仰有关的民间习俗。

总之，十二生肖作为中华民族文化传统中一种特定的精神文化现象。它通俗易懂，生动有趣，得以保留至今，成为了

宝贵的非物质文化遗产。在现代社会,十二生肖文化已经演化成一种不可取代的民族符号和精神象征。

Folk Traditions about Chinese Zodiac

  Folk activities about Chinese zodiac are varied and rich. Majorly they are seasonal activities, social etiquettes, clothing and entertainment, food and drink. Due to the changes in social lifestyle, the ethnic group and geographical differences, these

activities vary in contents and forms.

In the Qing Dynasty, there was a holiday named "Warehouse Fulfilling Holiday", when the merchants who sold rice prayed to the rat, "the god of the warehouse". According to *Notes about Seasons in Beijing* by Pan Rongsheng, "It was near the Warehouse Fulfilling Holiday, the warehouses were empty, and we should put in crops to refill them." At the night of the holiday, people should not light up, in order not to interfere with the marriage of the rats. At the day when the rats got married, people fried soybeans and blended these with brown sugar, and put these soybeans in the corners of their houses.

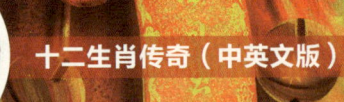
十二生肖传奇（中英文版）

Different places had different traditions about the day. Some people scattered salt and rice in the house corners. They called it "share the money with rats". Some people steamed 12 dough rats without eyes on the 14th day of the first month in lunar calendar, and served them as tributes on the 15th, the Lantern Festival, to pray for the rats leaving their crops alone.

"Whipping the oxen in spring" was popular in recent years in rural areas, also known as "whipping the spring", to boost farming and announce the beginning of the new-year labor. Farmers put five kinds of crops into a paper-made ox, whipped it and scattered the crops, symbolizing "all crops flowing with a wonderful harvest". Back in the Qing Dynasty, the officials distributed *The Picture of Spring Ox and the "God of Crops"* to the farmers. In the picture, colors of all parts of the ox as well as the age, dress and position of the "God of Crops" were designed according to the relationship of the Heavenly and Earthly Branches of the year, and that of the five elements and yin-yang. The picture also served as an almanac.

In many places, cloth toy tigers are popular. People think tigers are gods who protect children. So the children wear hats and shoes with tiger sign. In this way, they were thought to be protected by the Tiger God. Uncles give nephews tiger-shaped pillows as presents on their birthdays. In some provinces uncles present nephews with yellow cloth tigers, when the nephews reach one year old and break off the tigers' tails when passing the threshold, meaning "to throw away the hardships (*kanke, kan* means threshold)". Children from some ethnic groups wear tiger claws and teeth to drive away the evil spirits. From the Zhou Dynasty to the Han Dynasty, people drew tigers on their gates as their "God of the Door" to protect their houses. The people in northern parts of China used to have a kind of New Year Picture named "Picture of the Godly Tiger Protecting the House", saying "The godly tiger comes down from a high mountain it dwells, into human world it casts the holy spell. After the good people buy this picture, in all seasons they will live safe and well."

Traditions about dragons dated back long. The "Dragon-Head-Raising Day" on the 2nd day of the 2nd month in the lunar calendar, was deemed to be the time when the crouching dragon was raising its head, so more rain came. People had

十二生肖传奇（中英文版）

their hair dressed on the day to gain the spirit like the dragon. Northern people made a string with straws and colored paper and hanged it on the beam, calling it "the string of the dragon tail". They ate noodles, baked pancakes and dumplings on this day, for these food looked like dragon whiskers, scales and ears. Besides, the Chinese have dragon-related festivals every month, such as the "dragon sacrificing festival" of the Yao Ethnic Group of Yunnan Province in the 1st month in the lunar calendar; the "dragon king sacrificing festival" of Shandong Province in the 3rd month; the fair of Leiyin Temple of Datong

City, Shanxi Province in the 4th month; the "Dragon Division Festival" of Jiaxing City, Zhejiang Province in the 5th month; "Bask the Dragon Costume" in the 6th month; the "Dragon Girl Temple Fair" in the 7th month, etc.

The northern nomadic groups were in the worship of horse. A legend named "snow-white horse god" was told in Bao'an Ethnic Group. The Dawo'er Ethnic Group called the horse god "Wengu", which was not allowed to be ridden by females. The Man Ethnic Group also consecrated the horse god.

A goat with one horn named "Xiezhi" in the ancient legends is the assistant of Gao Yao, the god of jurisdiction. Wang Chong said in *Lun Heng*, Chapter Shiying, "When Gao Yao made the judgment, Xiezhi knocked the suspects over when they were guilty, and left them unscathed when they were not."

Up to now, the saying of "year of one's own animal" have been still popular. People also call it "year of one's Chinese zodiac", which means the year represented by the same animal with that of the year they were born in, met by one in every 12 years. It was said that "in this year, you are in conflict with the

Jupiter (*Taisui* in ancient Chinese), and there will be troubles instead of happiness." The year of one's Chinese zodiac is thought to be lacking in luck, so it is also called "the year of vicissitudes". Traditions about wearing red to avoid evil things in this year are prevalent all over China. Everyone, old and young, changes into red underwear, red belt and other red decorations like red scarf or necklace, in the day before the year of their Chinese zodiac, which is called "the red of one's own animal". In some places, on the night of this day, people should not go out; a married man should be accompanied by ladies.

Ancient people valued names very much. They thought names should make up for the luck, and the Chinese zodiac is an important reference for naming. Zou Yinglong, a litterateur in the Song Dynasty, was born on the hour of *Ren* (Dragon) in the eighth year of Qiandao, so he was named Yinglong (*long* means dragon). Tang Bohu, a famous artist in the Ming Dynasty, was said to be born on the hour, month and year of *Yin* (tiger), so he was named Tang Yin. People used to give their children "lower" pet names, and they thought in this way the children would be raised easily. Shu Qingchun (pen name Lao

She), a famous writer, had a pet name of "little dog tail", for he was born on the year of dog. The painter Ye Qianyu's pet name was "A Yang (goat)".

People of Han Ethnic Group used pigs for all the great sacrificing activities, and the head of the pig was the most valued. Wu Guren said in *Miscellaneous Poems of the New Year*, "It is a tradition of the Hangzhou City to use pig head for sacrificing… Choose the ones with wrinkles like a character *shou* (long life), named 'pig head with *Shou* character'." Up to now people in Zhejiang Province still make pickled pig head as the "new year purchases" in the last month of the lunar year.

十二生肖传奇（中英文版）

On Tomb Sweeping Festival some people used roast pigs to consecrate their ancestors The proverb "the ancestors distribute the pork to everyone" means that the whole family can eat the sacrifices after the rite. In the old times, some people would have the elderly set up a table for burning incense when severe disasters happened to the family, for beating the "sow ghost". The saying was "kill a sow ghost and drive away an evil spirit". They would pick a lucky day, kill an old sow and put its entrails inside of the house. After the sacrifice they ate these entrials.

十二生肖文化漫谈

People have other traditions about Chinese zodiac in marriage, agriculture, character or the destiny of the nation.

In a word, Chinese zodiac is a specific culture enjoyed by the Chinese in their traditions. It was easy to understand, and interesting to practice, so it was passed down till today and became a precious non-material cultural heritage. In the modern society, it has turned into an irreplaceable ethnic symbol and spiritual token.

第二部分
十二生肖的传奇

Part Two
The Legends of Twelve Zodiac Animals

鼠的传奇

鼠在十二生肖中居于首位，与十二地支中的"子"相配。晚上十一点至次日凌晨一点，属"子时"，正是老鼠趁夜深人静，频繁活动之时，故老鼠又称"子鼠"。因为老鼠繁殖力强，而古人又祈求生命繁衍、子孙兴旺，于是，民间就有了敬奉

十二生肖的传奇

"子神"的习俗。

老鼠被人们认为比较聪明,爱动脑筋。一些地方还把老鼠作为财富的象征,对老鼠崇拜有加。

传奇一:只因爱闻此香气　飞鼠奋勇保名药

在神农架一带有这样的传说:当药农发现峭壁上长有金钗石斛而悬绳采摘时,常常会从树林里或岩洞中突然飞出一只脸像狸、眼睛似猫、嘴巴像鼠、耳朵似兔、前爪锋利、全身的毛为棕褐色的飞鼠。它会扑向药农上方的绳索,并将之咬断,使药农葬身山谷。飞鼠之所以要咬断绳索致药农于死地,是因为它特别爱闻金钗石斛散发出的香气。

传奇二:黄鼠共贮御冬粮　恩爱夫妻似人间

北方有一种小黄鼠,实行严格的一夫一妻制,洞穴中的小土窑,好似床榻一般,这就是它们的婚床。平日里,它们共同准备御冬的食物,分别放进小土窑贮存起来。每当天气晴朗时,它们坐在洞口,看见人来,则拱动前脚,好像"作揖"一样,随时准备逃回洞穴中。因此,人们又称它为"礼鼠"。

十二生肖传奇（中英文版）

The Legend of Rat

The rat ranks the first among the twelve animals in Chinese zodiac. It is associated with the *Zi* in the Twelve Earthly Branches and the hours from 11:00 p.m. to 1:00 a.m. This is the time when the rat goes out most frequently, covered by the night. Therefore it is also referred to as "Rat of *Zi*". Rats are fertile, and the ancient people wished for a thriving family with lots of offspring to carry down the line. So the folks consecrated "the God of *Zi* (rat)".

The rat is considered to be smart and quick in mind, and in some places, a sign of wealth to worship.

Legend 1: Flying Rats Bravely Protect Herbs for Its Favorate Scent

A story is told in Shennongjia of Hebei that a kind of flying rat often fought with local herb collectors. When these collectors pick up dendrobium stems on the cliffs, some rats

with palm civet's face, cat's eyes, rat's mouth, rabbit's ears, sharp claws and brown fur, rushed out all of a sudden from woods or craves, and bit off their ropes. Sometimes the farmers would fall down the cliff after the rats' attack. The reason was the kind of flying rats loved the smell of dendrobium stems, and wanted to keep them from the collectors.

Legend 2: Yellow Rat Couple Store Food Together for Winter, Who Says Love Is Only Between Human

A yellow rat in the north performs strict monogamy. They live in caves, and utilize the mud humps in the caves as their wedding bed. They find food for winter in other seasons, and

store it in the mud hump. In sunny days they sit in front of their caves, fold their front feet together and wave them when seeing others come, like bowing, to prepare for running back to the cave. With that behavior, they are also called "the rat of courtesy".

牛的传奇

牛在十二生肖中居于第二位，与十二地支中的"丑"相配。凌晨一点至三点，属"丑时"。这时候的牛吃足了草，正在享受反刍的过程，故称"丑牛"。因为牛耕，中国人对牛感情渐深，把憨厚勤劳、不求回报等优秀品质附加在牛身上，鲁迅先生就以"俯首甘为孺子牛"言志。

在古代，牛是最尊贵的祭祀品，供天子祭祀社稷和天地专用。春秋战国的诸侯会盟，国君执牛耳割出血，涂在嘴边。

哈尼族的创世神话《奥色密色》，记载着牛的各部分化作自然万物的故事。汉族地区崇拜牛王，成都就有始建于康熙七年（1668年）的牛王庙。在很多地方水牛角、黄牛角、牦牛角等是最常见门上装饰之一。藏族人挂牛角于门上，牛角的多少象征捕猎水平的高低，甚至打扮穿衣都以牛角作为饰物。

传奇一：老黄牛嗜酒如命　不给酒喝不干活

广东省清新县的一头老黄牛嗜酒如命，一天不喝一瓶酒，它就犁不了田，耕不了地。

负责饲养这头牛的刘老汉认为牛喝酒之事不足为奇。在他的老家广西，每年都会举行几次斗牛比赛，为了激发牛的斗志，往往都要给牛适量的酒喝。"但是不能给多了，喝多了牛也会发酒疯，满地里跑，人就控制不住了。"在刘老汉的记忆中，最能喝酒的黄牛每次能喝3～4瓶50多度的白酒，而水牛甚至能喝7～8瓶。

传奇二：印尼有牛叫里贝　帮人渡河作工具

印度尼西亚有一种叫"里贝"的牛，体型比一般牛大，四肢极为粗壮，泅水能力很强。它泅水时，背部露出水面十分

平稳。当地人在牛背上绑上一个不漏水的方形木盘,让人坐在上面,作为渡河的交通工具。

The Legend of Ox

Ox ranks the second among the twelve animals in Chinese zodiac. It is associated with *Chou* in the Twelve Earthly Branches and the hours from 1:00 a.m. to 3:00 a.m. This is the time when the ox has eaten enough grass and is enjoying its rumination. Therefore it is also referred to as "Ox of *Chou*". Chinese people have deep affection to the ox, for it has worked for the farmers for a long time. People attach merits such as honesty, diligence and selflessness to it. Lu Xun once marked his own aspiration as "Head bowed, like a willing ox I serve the children".

In the ancient times, oxen were the most sacred sacrifices, only used during the emperor's rites to pay tribute to the society, heaven and earth. In the Spring and Autumn Period and the Warring States Period, on the meetings of the dukes and princes, the emperor cut the ox ear and rub the blood into his own mouth. *Aosemise*, a genesis mythology of Hani Ethnic Group, recorded a story about the parts of an ox turning into all the things in nature. The Han People worshipped the ox king, and there is an ox king temple in Chengdu City, Sichuan Province, built in the seventh year of the Emperor Kangxi of the Qing Dynasty. Horns of buffalo, cattle and yak were the most commonly seen decorations on the gate. People of the Zang Ethnic Group often hanged horns on the gates to show their hunting skills, and used horns to decorate their clothing.

Legend 1: Tippler Ox Go on Strike Without Liquor

In Qingxin County, Guangdong Province, an ox was addicted to the liquor and refused to work without it.

Old Liu was taking care of the ox. He knew that other oxen had drunk liquor before in his hometown, Guangxi Province, the matadors fed oxen liquor on the bull-fighting contests every year. "You shouldn't give them too much to drink, or they will go mad and run around, and you will lose

十二生肖的传奇

control of them." In his memory, each cattle could drink 3~4 bottles of liquor which contained more than 50% of alcohol; while each buffalo, 7~8 bottles.

Legend 2: Indonesia Libey Oxen Help People Cross River as Major Transportation Means

In Indonesia, a kind of ox named Libey is larger than other oxen. They have strong legs, and are very good at walking in the water. When it is crossing a river, its back keeps steady above the water. The local people tie a large water-proof square wooden plate to its back, so it can carry people across the rivers, as a major transportation means.

十二生肖传奇（中英文版）

虎的传奇

虎在十二生肖中居于第三位，与十二地支中的"寅"相配。凌晨三点至五点，属"寅时"。此时老虎最活跃、最凶猛，山林里，常会在此时听到虎啸声，故称"寅虎"。在中国，老虎自古就被认为是"兽中之王"，它高贵、凶猛，受人敬畏和崇拜。白虎是中国道教的四大守护神之一。在《礼记·曲礼上》就有"前朱雀，后玄武，左青龙，右白虎"的说法。土家

族多信奉白虎神。

在民间各种礼仪和节日活动中,很多与虎有关的事项,多与巫术有关。陕西黄陵县的青年结婚时,婆家要捏面塑的四对虎馍和兔馍,馍内分别放入核桃、红枣、钱,名叫"硬盘盘",也叫"夫妻花馍"。男方到女方接亲时,放到娘家两对,当众掰开,若先掰出核桃,便预示先生男孩,先掰出红枣,预示先生女孩。这些婚俗巫术和占卜巫术,经过时光的锤炼,已逐步演化成民间的习俗。

传奇一:虎狗相伴近十年　相濡以沫情谊浓

1991年,四川省自贡市动物园从南京动物园买了一只东北公虎崽。由于虎崽离开虎妈妈和与它朝夕相处的兄弟,所以一直打不起精神。于是,动物园按虎崽的个头,在宠物集市上购买了一条黄色四川公土狗作为它的伙伴。虎崽和土狗互相对峙了半个小时后,相互用嘴巴嗅了嗅对方的脑门,就一起玩耍起来。

虎崽长大后,动物园安排其和母虎配种,进展不顺,便又将土狗"请"来作陪,帮助它的"朋友"和母虎成功"恋爱"。100多天后,母虎顺利产下了两只小虎崽。

十二生肖传奇（中英文版）

传奇二：秦岭猛虎善牧羊 "食一儆百"吓群羊

秦岭虎有个贮备食物的绝招——牧羊而食。岩羊常常结伴而行，秦岭虎则瞅准时机，猛然而出，厉声咆哮，吓得群羊不敢动弹。如有敢逃跑者，秦岭虎就将其咬得鲜血淋漓，杀一儆百，吓得其余岩羊老老实实，甘当"俘虏"。这只"牧羊虎"则押着羊群，到寻不到食物时，便生吞一只。

The Legend of Tiger

Tiger ranks the third among the twelve animals in Chinese zodiac. It is associated with *Yin* in the Twelve Earthly Branches and the hours from 3:00 a.m. to 5:00 a.m. This is the time when the tigers are the most excited and ferocious, roaring in the forest. Therefore it is also referred to as "Tiger of *Yin*". Throughout Chinese history, the tiger is thought to be "the king of the woods". It incited a sense of both awe and worship for its power and ferocity. Tiger is one of the four guardian gods of Taoism. "Chapter of Propriety" Part One in *The Book of Rites*

records, "(Banner with the) Red Bird should be in the front, that with the Black Tortoise behind, that with the Azure Dragon on the left, and that with the White Tiger on the right". The Tujia Ethnic Group worshiped white tigers as the god of family.

In all kinds of rituals and festival activities, many issues about tigers relate with witchcraft. In Huangling County of Shaanxi Province, the groom's family will prepare four pairs of steamed buns in the shapes of tiger and rabbit, filled with walnuts, dates and coins, named "wedding *huamo*", featuring a bridal couple. When the groom pick up his bride on the

wedding day, two pairs of the *huamo* will be presented to the bride's family and broken apart in public. If the walnut filling occurs first, the bridal couple's first baby will be a boy; and the date filling, a girl. These wedding traditions and superstitions evolve into folk customs over time.

Legend 1: A Tiger and a Dog: Deep Friendship for a Decade

In 1991, a zoo in Zigong City of Sichuan Province bought a male Manchurian tiger cub. It was sad after leaving its mother and brothers. Therefore the zoo bought a yellow rural male dog with the size of the tiger cub to keep it company. The first half an hour witnessed a confrontation between the two; while then, they sniffed each other's head and began to play together.

After the tiger grew up, the zoo coupled it with a female tiger for breeding. When the relationship went rough, the dog was invited to accompany the tiger. And its relationship with the "bride" turned better. After 100 days, the "bride" gave birth to two cubs smoothly.

Legend 2: Qinling Mountain Tiger Flocks and Preys, Leaving Sheep in Deep Terror

The Qinling tigers have a unique way of preying: they both flock and prey on sheep. When bharals graze in the Qinling Mountain, the tiger comes out of a sudden and roar loudly to freeze the sheep by terror. Any sheep who dare run away will be bitten and eaten by the tiger, so the rest are scared straight, and captured. The tiger drives the herd everywhere, and tends to kill one in the herd when wild prey is scare.

兔的传奇

兔在十二生肖中居于第四位,与十二地支中的"卯"相配。凌晨五点至七点,属"卯时"。这时候,月亮的余晖还没完全隐退,而玉兔是月亮的代称,故称"卯兔"。天刚亮,也是兔子出窝觅食青草的好时光。作为承载祥和愿望的生肖,兔子也不例外,被寄托了诸多美好寓意。虽然在传统意象中,有关兔子的成语、俗语,贬义居多,但民俗也在承袭中不断被赋予新的内涵,走进新时代的兔子,早已成为"动如脱兔""'兔'飞猛进"式的吉兽。

四川盆地有仙兔盗酒为娘亲疗伤,成就一段美好姻缘的传说。据说古时候四川盆地有个小伙子开酒坊,有一天夜里,撞见一只雪白的兔子在偷自家的枸杞酒。小伙子不仅没有责怪,反而将酒送给了它。几天后,一绝美少女抱着酒坛来到他家,说是酿了好酒请他尝。两人互生情愫,从此结下姻缘。原来这少女便是那只仙兔化身,当日偷酒是为了救治自己的娘亲。

十二生肖的传奇

传奇一：兔子求偶闹邻居　法庭判建隔音屏

伦敦有位妇女家里饲养了三十多只兔子，某年的春天，正值兔子的"求偶"年龄。在此期间，兔子们交配不分早晚，吵得邻居无法休息。邻居无奈，将养兔子的妇女告上法庭。这位妇女在法庭上振振有词："兔子求偶是自然现象，应给予保护。"最后，法庭令她立即在花园里安装隔音屏障，不要再让邻居受到干扰，否则，她将受到重罚。

十二生肖传奇（中英文版）

传奇二：兔子五年学抽烟　定时要抽五支烟

坐落在美国西海岸的一家医学科研所,有一只名叫"凯尔"的兔子。实验人员把凯尔的房间作为抽烟室,还教凯尔抽烟。经过五年的熏陶,凯尔终于学会了抽烟。由于染上烟瘾,现在,它每天要定时抽五支烟。抽烟时,凯尔嘴里叼着烟卷,神情专注、自在。要是迟一会给它烟抽,它就会发怒,表现出烦躁不安。

The Legend of Rabbit

The rabbit ranks the fourth among the twelve animals in Chinese zodiac. It is associated with *Mao* in the Twelve Earthly Branches and the hours from 5:00 a.m. to 7:00 a.m. At this time the moon has not faded completely, and rabbit stands for the moon because there is said to be a Jade Rabbit living on the moon. Therefore it is also referred to as "Rabbit of *Mao*". And it is also the time when the rabbits come out of their holes and graze on dewed fresh grass. The rabbit is a tame creature representing loads of good wishes as one of Chinese zodiac. In the traditional sense, the idioms of rabbits are mostly negative, while new meanings are also given to the animal: vigorous like a rabbit; advance like a rabbit.

A beautiful story shared in Sichuan Basin tells a rabbit fairy stole the wine to cure her mother, which led to a happy and wonderful marriage. A young man had a liquor workshop in the Sichuan Basin, and one night he ran into a snow-white rabbit trying to steal his medlar wine. He didn't blame the rabbit, but gave away the wine. A few days later a beautiful maiden came to his house with a jar of wine for him. They fell in love with each other after and got married. The maiden turned out to be the rabbit who took on human form and fell in love with the man to pay a debt of gratitude for giving her the medlar wine the other day, which was for curing her mother.

Legend 1: Owner Sued for Noises Made by Rabbit Mating

A lady in London raised more than 30 rabbits, and when

it was spring, the "love noises" made by the rabbits drove the neighbors restless. So they sued the lady, who responded on the court by "the mating of the rabbits is natural, so it should be protected". At last, the court sentenced her to set up a noise-proof screen in her garden, or she would be punished more severely.

Legend 2: Rabbit Smokes 5 Cigarettes a Day after 5-Year Learning

A medical research institution in the western coast of the

U.S. had a rabbit named Kyle. It lived in the smoking room, and was taught to smoke by the staff. After five years it learned to smoke, and was even addicted to it. Each day it had to smoke 5 cigarettes. With a cigarette in the mouth, it felt absorbed and at ease; if anyone took the cigarette away, it would be upset and anxious.

十二生肖传奇（中英文版）

龙的传奇

龙在十二生肖中居于第五位，与十二地支中的"辰"相配。早晨七点至九点，属"辰时"。龙是神话中的动物，传说龙喜欢在旭日东升时腾云驾雾，故称"辰龙"。

龙是中华民族的图腾，也是中国文化的象征。在中国文化中，龙不仅是拥有呼风唤雨之力的神兽，而且也被视为吉祥瑞兽。从距今八千多年的新石器时代，先民们就崇拜龙的图腾。到今天，人们仍然多以带有"龙"字的成语或典故来形容生活中的美好事物，如"龙腾虎跃""龙

十二生肖的传奇

马精神"等。中国人还自豪地称自己是"龙的传人",所以,"龙"也就成了中华民族的象征和符号。

传说在帝舜的时候,董父因擅于驯养龙,故被赐予氏族名"豢龙氏"。夏代也有驯养龙的人叫刘累,被赐予氏族名"御龙氏"。从这些传说看,至少从尧舜禹时期,民间就有了龙的传说故事。数千年来,中国龙的形象有这样一个演变过程:新石器时代简单质朴的"原龙",夏商周时期神秘抽象的"夔龙",春秋战国与秦汉时期粗犷雄健的"飞龙",魏晋隋唐刚柔并济的"行龙",宋元明清复杂华丽的"黄龙",当代吉庆嘉瑞的"祥龙"。

传奇一:龙口山泉神酒美　皇帝赐名为"龙酒"

据说唐朝时,东北地区有座龙脊山,山脚下有一个老龙口山泉。一对中年夫妇用老龙口山泉的水酿造出了口感绵软甘甜的美酒,献给玄宗皇帝品尝。唐玄宗尝后赞此酒为"神酒",并令御医又添加了十余种上好的御用食材,酿造出了更加醇美的御用"龙酒"。

传奇二:轩辕铸鼎荆山下　鼎湖乘龙见天帝

据传在上古洪荒时代,秦岭之北、荆山(现河南省灵宝

十二生肖传奇（中英文版）

市阳平镇）脚下有一湖泊，因黄帝在此汲水铸鼎而名曰"鼎湖"。当轩辕黄帝历经千辛万苦铸造出第一个鼎的时候，天上突然飞下来一条龙。那条龙的眼睛威武有神，长长的龙须银光闪烁。它降临时，天空霞光万丈，湖水泛着金光，大地笼罩在耀眼的光芒之中。原来，天帝对黄帝造福百姓的举动非常欣慰，派这条龙前来接黄帝去天庭。黄帝欣然应邀。只见金龙一声长啸，载着黄帝直冲云霄，瞬间就消失在云雾之中。

The Legend of Dragon

Dragon ranks the fifth among the twelve animals in Chinese zodiac. It is associated with *Chen* in the Twelve Earthly Branches and the hours from 7:00 a.m. to 9:00 a.m. The legendary dragon is said to like to ride on the mists and clouds at sunrise. Therefore it is also referred to as "Dragon of *Chen*".

Dragon is the totem of China as well as its symbol. Chinese deem that dragon is the god-like beast standing for luck, which can also control rain and wind. In the Neolithic

age 8,000 years ago, the ancient people worshiped the totem of dragon; up to now, people still use many phrases including the word "dragon" to describe good things in their lives, such as "dragons rising and tigers leaping" "the vigor of dragons and horses". Chinese call themselves proudly "Descendant of the Dragon". Thus dragon became a symbol of our nation.

It is said that when Emperor Shun ruled in the ancient times, a man named Dong Fu was given a clan name "Huanlong" for his superb ability of taming dragons. In the Xia Dynasty, a man named Liu Lei was given a clan name "Yulong", also for skills in training dragons. According to these legends, fantasy stories about dragons dated from Yao, Shun and Yu

十二生肖传奇（中英文版）

Period. In the thousands of years, there was an evolutionary progress about the image of dragons: simple "original dragon" in the Neolithic age; mysterious "Kui dragon" in the Xia, Shang and Zhou Dynasties; rough and masculine "flying dragon" in Spring and Autumn Periods, Warring States Period, the Qin and the Han Dynasties; both forceful and soft "moving dragon" in the Wei, Jin, Sui and Tang Dynasties; complicated and gorgeous "yellow dragon" in the Song, Yuan, Ming and Qing Dynasties; and the "lucky dragon" symbolizing good fortune in the recent periods.

Legend 1: Fine Wine Made of Longkou Mountain Spring and Named "Dragon Wine" by the Emperor

It was said that in the Tang Dynasty, there was a "Dragon Ridge Mountain" in the northeastern region of China, with a spring named "Old Dragon Mouth". A middle-aged couple made sweet and soft wine with the spring water, and gave it as tribute to Emperor Xuanzong. The Emperor was greatly impressed and named it "the godly wine". He asked the royal doctors to add more than ten rare ingredients into the wine, and made a more intoxicating "dragon wine" to serve as one of the royal drinks.

Legend 2: Yellow Emperor Ride a Dragon to Visit the Jade Emperor

It was said that in the times of great antiquity, there was a lake under Mountain Jin, north of the Qinling Mountains (now in Yangping Town of Baoling City of Henan Province). It was named "*Ding* Lake" for the Yellow Emperor was making *Ding* (a giant vessel for cooking or holding water) with its water. When the first one was made, suddenly a dragon came down from the heaven. It had mighty blinking eyes, its whiskers blinking with silver light. When it arrived, the lake shined the light of gold, and all the earth was in bright light. It turned out that the Jade Emperor was glad about the Yellow Emperor's efforts to benefit people, and sent the dragon to take him. The Yellow Emperor agreed gladly, and jumped on the dragon. The dragon gave a long roar, flew into the sky, and then disappeared in the clouds.

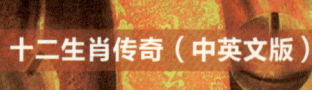

十二生肖传奇(中英文版)

 的传奇

蛇在十二生肖中居于第六位,与十二地支中的"巳"相配。上午九点至十一点,属"巳时"。这时候,大雾散去,艳阳高照,蛇多躲藏在草丛中休息,故称"巳蛇"。

蛇是自然界最古老、生命力极强的动物之一,是居住在长江中下游地区汉民族的主要图腾。一些地方忌讳对家蛇直呼其名,而是称作"苍龙""小龙"或"仙家",唯恐对其不敬而惹祸。此禁忌习俗源于人们对蛇的崇拜信仰,人们相信蛇可福佑于人。

十二生肖的传奇

传奇一：非洲丛林一旅馆　人身缠蛇为避暑

在非洲的丛林中生活着一种无毒的蛇，它们喜欢与人为伍，从不伤人，人也喜欢它们。由于丛林酷热，它缠在人身上时，人会感到非常凉爽舒适。有人在丛林中开设了一个旅馆，其特色就在于每个房间都提供这种蛇，旅客可以让它们缠绕在身上作避暑之用。

传奇二：相濡以沫二十载　人蛇相处两依依

20世纪80年代初，四川省眉山市仁寿县居民唐某家的简陋草房里出现了一条白底黑花的大蛇。那蛇身有茶杯般粗，盘着如一个米筛那么大。唐某想，蛇本是民间吉祥之物，不能随便猎杀，便听之任之。此后，蛇也就不客气地住了下来。它不仅没有惹是生非，反倒捕食老鼠，让唐家免于鼠患。后来唐某推倒草房、兴建新房，大蛇就"隐居"在新房的屋顶上。它在唐家住了20年之久，体型越长越大，性格十分温顺。

十二生肖传奇（中英文版）

The Legend of Snake

The snake ranks the sixth among the twelve animals in Chinese zodiac. It is associated with *Si* in the Twelve Earthly Branches and the hours from 9:00 a.m. to 11:00 a.m. At the time, the morning fog has gone, and the sun shines brightly. The snake hides inside of the grass to rest. Therefore it is also referred to as "Snake of Si".

The snake is one of the most ancient and vital animals in nature. It is a major feature of the totem of Han clan living in the middle and lower reaches of the Yangtze River. In some places, it is a taboo to call snake by its name. People refer to them as "the blue dragon" "the little dragon" or "the fairy", to avoid troubles from disrespect to the animal. People worship the snakes and think they could bring people fortune.

Legend 1: Guests Served by Snakes in African Jungle Hotel for Cooling

A snake hotel in an African jungle is world's unique. There is a kind of non-poisonous snakes, which are friends of people, and never hurt people. When the snakes twist on human body, people feel cool and comfortable. So someone opened a hotel in the jungle, offering a snake of such kind to the guests

for keeping cool.

Legend 2: 20-Year Friendship Between a Villager and a Snake

In the early 1980s, a villager named Tang in Sichuan Basin region had a shallow thatched hut. One day a big white snake with black spots came to his house. It was as thick as a mug, and as big as a rice sieve when it curled up. Tang thought that snake was the lucky animal according to the tradition and shouldn't be killed, so he let it stay in the house. The snake didn't cause any trouble in the house, but helped Tang's family to avoid the rat trouble. When Tang became richer and planned to tear down the thatched hut and built a new one, it lived on the beam of his new house like a hermit. It lived with Tang for more than 20 years, with a growing body but a tamed temperament.

十二生肖的传奇

马的传奇

马在十二生肖中居于第七位,与十二地支的"午"相配。上午十一点至下午一点,属"午时"。中午时分,阳气达到极点,阴气渐渐增加,在阴阳交替之时,一般动物都躺着休息了,马却还习惯站着,故称"午马"。

马是人类历史上最早饲养的动物之一,人们认为马具有勤劳、勇敢和忠诚的品质。无论是在农耕、狩猎、战争,还是

十二生肖传奇（中英文版）

运输方面,马都是人类重要的伙伴。

传奇一：丢失三天小女孩　遮风供暖有义马

在哈萨克斯坦共和国的一家国营农场,一位四岁的女孩在和小伙伴们玩耍时迷路了。三天后,附近牧民发现,在一条河渠的岸边,有三匹马围成一个三角形,而一个小女孩躺在它们中间的凹地上。三匹马用力呼吸着,为她供暖。女孩恢复知觉后告诉人们,她迷路后遇到的这三匹马始终没有离开过她,为她遮风和供暖,与她一起共度了近三昼夜,使她得以活下来。

传奇二：舍生取义救马群　集体主义好典范

在广袤无垠的内蒙古大草原,午时的阳光暖洋洋的,一群马正在悠闲地吃着青草。为防止敌兽的侵害,几匹健壮的马总是站在外围担任警戒。突然,一群野狼向马群飞奔而来,担任警戒的马一声长啸,掩护马群逃跑。然而,大群野狼紧追不放。这时,只见正在奔跑的马群中,有一匹马自动倒下牺牲自己,以保卫同伴脱险。可是,仍有许多野狼在追赶它们。不一会,又有一匹马倒在地上自我牺牲。野狼的数量实在太多了,十几只精疲力竭的马终于停了下来,并很快围成

十二生肖的传奇

一个圆圈。几十只野狼迅速把马群包围起来,只见几匹身强力壮的马主动站在外围,头朝里,脚朝外,猛踢上前的野狼,保护老弱病残的马。战斗一直持续到夜幕降临,马群在搏斗中,又失去了两匹同伴,才从野狼的围困中逃脱。

The Legend of Horse

The horse ranks the seventh among the twelve animals in Chinese zodiac. It is associated with *Wu* in the Twelve Earthly Branches and the hours from 11:00 a.m. to 1:00 p.m. At the noon, *Yangqi* (positive energy) has reached its mount, and *Yinqi* (negative energy) is beginning to accumulate. At this time, the alternation of *Yin* and *Yang* makes most animals lie down and nap, while only the horse stands. Therefore it is also referred to as "Horse of *Wu*".

The horse is the earliest animal bred by people. They are considered to have the merits of diligence, bravery and loyalty. They are people's close companions, no matter in agriculture,

hunting, warfare or transportation.

Legend 1: A Missing 4-Year-Old Girl Kept Alive by Loyal Horses for 3 days

On a state-funded farm in the Republic of Kazakhstan, a four-year-old girl lost her way when playing with her friends. Three days later she was found lying in a piece of hollow ground, on the bank of a river, with three horses forming a triangle around her. The horses breathed with force to give her warmth. After she woke up she told that the horses never left her and sheltered her since she was found by them. She might not have survived without them.

Legend 2: Horses Sacrifice Themselves to Save the Herd, a Great Model for Collectivism

In the vast prairie of Inner Mongolia, the sun shone warmly, and a herd of horses were grazing with ease. A few strong horses were standing outside to guard the herd in case of the attack from other beasts. Suddenly a pack of wild wolves rushed to them. The guard neighed long and loudly to cover the herd running away. Yet the wolves persisted in pursuing. At the time, one of the horses lay down to feed the wolves and let others run; Another did the same then, for there were still many wolves chasing them. The number of the wolves was so large that the left horses finally stopped running for tiredness and formed a circle, and the large pack of wolves surrounded them. A few strong horses stood on the outskirt of the herd, and kicked the wolves to protect the old and weak. The battle continued to the midnight, and the horses lost two more members, and managed to escape from the wolves.

十二生肖传奇(中英文版)

羊的传奇

羊在十二生肖中居于第八位,与十二地支中的"未"相配。午后一点至三点,属"未时"。这时候是放羊的好时机,故称"未羊"。

在民间有"羊羔跪乳"的传说,小羊为了感激母亲的养育之恩而下跪吃奶,蕴含着感恩父母、尊敬长辈的道理。羊是古代的吉祥物,象征祥瑞。

传奇一:山羊苦恋小公象　矢志不渝难分离

当巴黎动物园的驯兽员让一只名叫"邓布尔"的母山羊与一头名叫"比利"的小公象作伴时,它们竟然成了难舍难分的伴侣。驯兽员奈莉说:"它们每天一起玩耍。"小象"比利"安闲地走着,而活泼的山羊"邓布尔"却一刻也闲不下来,它一会儿跳,一会儿跑。吃食时,如果把它们分开,它们谁也不肯吃东西。

传奇二：大漠奇观"羊上树" 采集坚果好帮手

如果你去摩洛哥西南部的撒哈拉大沙漠旅游,就会看到很多山羊,有的趴在树干上,有的站在树枝上。原来在当地,秋天来临时,食物变得稀缺,这里的山羊每天会花约四分之三的时间在当地特有的"阿甘树"上觅食。那里的牧羊人将羊群赶到树下,让它们爬上树吃果子。这些山羊一边咀嚼着

十二生肖传奇（中英文版）

阿甘果，一边在树枝之间来回跳跃。牧羊人会跟随在山羊后面，捡拾从山羊嘴里掉到地上的阿甘果核。然后把果核砸开，从中取出具有苦味的果仁，磨碎之后，榨出十分珍贵的阿甘油，用于烹调和制作化妆品等。如今，"羊上树"已成为了世界各地游客不可错过的独特景观，也给当地带来了可观的经济效益。

The Legend of Goat

The goat ranks the eighth among the twelve animals in Chinese zodiac. It is associated with *Wei* in the Twelve Earthly Branches and the hours from 1:00 p.m. to 3:00 p.m. This is the good timing for grazing, therefore it is also named the "Goat of *Wei*".

There is a Chinese saying, "goats know filial piety by kneeling down for nursing", which means lambs would kneel down on their front legs to suck ewe's milk. The story tells us to pay tribute to our parents and respect the elderly. The goat is

considered a mascot representing mercy and goodness.

Legend 1: Bitter and Persistent Love Between an Elephant and a Goat

When an animal trainer made a female goat named Danbury as companion to a small male elephant named Billy, they became inseparable lovers to everyone's surprise. Nelly, the trainer, said, "they played together every day." The little elephant Billy always walked peacefully while the playful goat Danbury never stopped jumping and running about. They

would both refuse to eat if they were separated in feeding.

Legend 2: Morocan Goats Grow on Trees and Help Make Argan Oil

If you travel to the Sahara Dessert in southwest Morocco, you can see many goats hanging out or standing lazily on tree branches. In this region, when autumn comes and the food sources turn scarce for wildlife, the goats will spend 3/4 of their time every day finding food on the famous "argania" (an indigenous tree). The local shepherds drive them near the arganias and the goats climb onto the trees for a good feed as soon as the fruit is ready. They sometimes jump about on the branches, and sometimes chew the argans on the tree. The shepherds follow them and pick up the argan nuts falling out of their mouths. Then people break the nuts open, take out the bitter-taste pips, grind them and extract precious argan oil for cooking or making cosmetic products. Nowadays, "tree-climbing goat" has become a unique scene to all the tourists coming from the whole world, and has brought large economic incomes as well.

猴的传奇

猴在十二生肖中居于第九位,与十二地支中的"申"相配。下午三点至五点,属"申时"。这时候,太阳已经偏西,猴子叫的声音最为洪亮,故称"申猴"。

在中国古代的传说中,"禺"就是一种猴子。它居住在树上,白面黑颊,多胡须而毛色斑斓。尾长过身,末端有分叉,雨天则用分叉的尾巴塞住鼻孔防止进水。爱群行,老的在前,少的在后。吃食相互推让,相爱而居,相聚而生,共同赴死。古人说它是"仁兽"。

索达吉堪布的佛学著作《悲惨世界》中的《母子情深》一文记载了这样一个故事:一个猎人,在森林中狩猎时,发现一群猴子,便开枪射击,结果打中一只母猴,其他猴子惊惶而逃。当他走近猎物时,发现母猴身边有一只小猴,正用舌头舔着母猴的伤口。猎人不禁思索,这只小猴不害怕吗?它面对猎人和死亡,为了照顾自己受伤的母亲,居然没有跑开。此时,母猴也护着小猴。那情景使他终生难忘。

十二生肖传奇(中英文版)

传奇一：长安山中猴放羊　报答老人好心肠

一年冬天，雪花纷飞，陕西省的黄培选夫妇正在自己家院中给羊喂苞谷，突然发现离他家不远处的山坡上有只马猴可怜巴巴地望着羊吃食。老两口忙招手呼唤猴子到院子觅食。这只猴子从此成为家里的一份子。黄家夫妇待猴子就像对自己的孩子一样。日子久了，猴子学会了放羊的本领。主人将羊圈打开，猴子就赶着六十多只羊上山，一边放羊一边吃野菜充饥。听到这对夫妇呼唤，就将羊赶回家。

十二生肖的传奇

传奇二：本州岛上一猴群　一夫一妻不变心

在日本本州岛上有一种猴群，实行一夫一妻制。即使是猴王也只能享有择偶的优先权，但只能一妻一妾，不能喜新厌旧，否则就会丢"官"，甚至丧命。"庶民"则实行严格的一夫一妻制度。雌猴感情专一，对"第三者"处处设防，若"第三者"献媚取宠，雌猴就会一边向其他同类"告发"，一边依偎在"丈夫"怀中。这时，猴群的首领便会当众责罚"第三者"。

The Legend of Monkey

The monkey ranks the ninth among the twelve animals in Chinese zodiac. It is associated with *Shen* in the Twelve Earthly Branches and the hours from 3:00 p.m. to 5:00 p.m. This is the moment when monkeys howl the most loudly; therefore it is also named "Monkey of *Shen*".

In the ancient legends of China, "Yu" was a kind of monkey. They lived in trees, with white face and black cheeks, whiskers and colorful fur. Their tails were longer than their bodies, and turned forked in the end, to stuff their nostrils for watertightness when raining. They loved to go out together, the old walking in front and the young behind. They shared their own food with others. They loved each other, lived together and died together. The ancients said they were "beasts with mercy".

Sodargye Khenpo's Buddhist work *A World of Misery* records a story "Love Between Mother and Son" that a hunter fired at a herd of monkeys in a forest and shot a female one, the rest fleeing. When he approached it, there was a baby monkey staying with its mother and licking its wound. "Is it afraid?" thought the hunter, "Surprisingly it didn't run away, and tried to take care of its mother." The mother tried to cover its child, too. The hunter was greatly impressed by the scene.

Legend 1: Grazing Monkey in Chang'an Mountain Requites the Old Couple's Favor

One snowy winter, Huang Peixuan and his wife of Shanxi Province were feeding the sheep in their yard when they found a monkey looking at them with sad eyes on the hillside close

to their house. The old couple waved to the monkey to let it in for food. From then on the monkey became a member of the family. The couple treated it like their child, and it learned how to graze after some days. When the couple opened the sheepfold, the monkey drove the sheep up to the hill to graze and ate some wild vegetables for food. When hearing the call of the couple, it drove the sheep back home.

Legend 2: Loyal Japanese Monkeys Stick to Monogamy and Never Change Heart

There was a monkey pack on Honshu Island of Japan that

honored the practice of monogamy. The monkey king enjoyed the sole priority in selecting partners but could possess only one wife and one concubine. He could not like the new and loathe the old, otherwise he might lose his position or even his life. The common monkeys strictly follow monogamy. The female monkeys were very devoted in affection and were always vigilant of a third party. If a "third wheel" made coquettish moves and tried to win favor, the "wife" would inform against the intruder to others and at the same time snuggle against the bosom of her husband. When this happened, the monkey king would punish the "third wheel" in public.

十二生肖的传奇

鸡的传奇

鸡在十二生肖中居于第十位,与十二地支中的"酉"相配。下午五点至七点,属"酉时"。这时候,太阳渐渐西落,鸡开始陆续回笼了,故称"酉鸡"。

鸡每天准时鸣叫,在人们心目中,是勤奋和守信的象征;同时,它还代表着新一天的到来,人们又有了新的希望。

民间有斗鸡的习俗。鸡在搏斗中,勇猛顽强,不畏流血,被人们当作英勇的典范。早在先秦时期,人们就有用鸡和鸡血驱鬼邪、去灾祸的活动。生活在江南地区的人们习惯大年初一在门上张贴鸡的图画,认为这样百鬼就不敢上门了。"杀鸡驱邪"至今仍是一些地区的风俗。

贵州省山区的苗族人有婚前"吃鸡酒"的习俗。在提亲当天,男方家会请人带两只红色羽毛的大公鸡到女方家,当众将它们宰杀,把两滴血滴到酒杯里混合后让男女双方饮下,表示相爱到老;鸡心、鸡肝、鸡肠子不切碎,按原样煮熟吃下,表示永不变心、永不分离。这时请德高望重的老人说一些吉利的话语,这就叫"吃鸡酒"。

传奇一:生死相恋两只鸡　此情绵绵无绝期

2000年春天,吉林省长春市两家住户饲养的公鸡和母鸡结为伴侣。公鸡对母鸡十分依恋,以至于不回自己家的笼子,晚上就在母鸡的笼子外席地而眠。公鸡的主人担心它被偷走,就不放它出门,它就整天大声啼叫、绝食,对主人表示抗议。后来,它为了和母鸡待在一起,偷跑出家门,甚至摔断了一条腿。主人无奈,只好杀了它。本以为它们的"爱情故事"就此结束,谁知几天后,主人发现那只和它"相好"的母鸡静静地趴在她家门口,大概是来寻找它的。母鸡每天都来静静地等候,直到某天在来的路上出了车祸,这只母鸡就这

样追随公鸡而去了。

传奇二：泰国曼谷一公鸡　文具店里好助手

泰国曼谷一家书报文具店养了一只叫"阿滑"的大公鸡。它每天凌晨 5 点即放声啼鸣，催促主人起床。吃过早餐后，店主把它放书报摊上，它就会精神抖擞地做"保安"的工作。若顾客需要购买书报，"阿滑"便会发出"咕咕"的叫声，店主闻声而来，将书报拿给顾客。若有人乱拿书报，"阿滑"就伸出利爪，把小偷抓得皮破血流。

The Legend of Rooster

The rooster ranks the tenth among the twelve animals in Chinese zodiac. It is associated with *You* in the Twelve Earthly Branches and the hours from 5:00 p.m. to 7:00 p.m. This is the sunset time, when the rooster goes back to its cage. Therefore it is also named "Rooster of *You*".

The rooster crows every morning on time, so it is a

 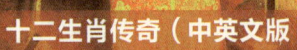

model of diligence and punctuality in people's mind. Also it represents a new day and a new hope. Cockfight is one of the folk traditions, in which people watch two cocks attack each other and bet on which one will win. Roosters were regarded as role-models of bravery and boldness in the fight, despite their bloodshed. In the early Qin Dynasty, rooster and its blood were believed to drive away the evil spirits. People who lived south of the Yangtze River put rooster pictures on the gate, and thought it would scare the ghosts away. And in some places

people still kill roosters to achieve the same effect.

People of Miao Ethnic Group in mountainous area in Guizhou Province have the tradition of "drinking rooster wine" before a marriage. On the wedding day, the groom's family will bring two red-feathered roosters to the bride's house, kill them in public, and put two drops of blood in the wine and make the new couple drink it, symbolizing their everlasting love. They do not cut the heart, liver and intestine of the roosters, instead they cook these ingredients as a whole and eat the dish, to show eternal love and no betrayal. At the time, some elderly with merits will say lucky words to bless the couple. This is called "drinking rooster wine".

Legend 1: A Rooster and a Hen Love Each Other in Life and Death

In the spring of 2000, a rooster "fell in love" with a hen raised by its neighbor, in Changchun City, Jilin Province. The rooster loved the hen so much that it did not return to its own cage at night, and slept right outside of the hen's cage. Its owner was afraid that it would be stolen, so he caged it. It crowed

loudly, and refused to eat all day for protest. Then it sneaked out of the house to see the hen, even at the cost of breaking one of its legs. The owner had to put it down, and thought its love story would end since then. Yet a few days later, its "wife" the hen squatted on the doorstep of its owner, presumably looking for the rooster. Every day since then it came, until it followed its "husband" to death after a car accident.

Legend 2: Rooster A'hua, a Great Shopkeeper in Stationary Store

The owner of a stationary store in Bangkok kept a rooster named A'hua, who crowed every morning at five to urge an early rising of its owner. The owner prepared the breakfast of the rooster, put it on the newspaper stand and went away for other businesses. It guarded the stand with a high spirit. If customers wanted newspaper or books, it clucked so that the owner would come out to cater for the customers. If anyone tried to steal something away, A'hua would use its claws to teach him a lesson.

十二生肖的传奇

狗的传奇

狗在十二生肖中居于第十一位,与十二地支中的"戌"相配。晚上七点至九点,属"戌时"。这时候,黑夜降临,人们劳碌一天,关门准备休息了。此时狗睡在各家门前,保护主人的安全,故称"戌狗"。

狗自古就有忠诚的美名。现代人对狗的喜爱尤甚,以"汪星人"称呼之。狗也是民间工艺美术品中经久不衰的题材,狗图案的年画、泥塑,以及布艺制品,一直为人们所喜爱。

十二生肖传奇（中英文版）

传奇一：少女飓风里遇难　义狗危难中施救

美国新泽西州海湾地区的狄克夫妇收养了一只漂亮的纯种纽芬兰狗，取名"维拉"。邻居安德逊家的十一岁小女孩安迪莉亚，每天放学回来都要过来同"维拉"一起玩。

1997年2月5日，飓风突然袭击了海湾，以每小时110公里的速度把正在玩雪的安迪莉亚刮到离海岸数米远的雪坑里。维拉找到了她，用自己热乎乎的大舌头拼命将她舔醒。然后，让安迪莉亚抱紧它的头颈后把她拖出了雪坑。突然，一阵飓风刮来，将安迪莉亚抛入大海。维拉毫不迟疑地跳进海水之中，咬住已快沉下去的安迪莉亚的衣服，奋力向岸边游去，最终它拖着女孩安全靠岸。

没多久，维拉的事迹传进了白宫。1997年12月26日，在圣诞节的庆祝活动上，时任美国第一夫人的希拉里授予了维拉一枚特别勋章。

传奇二：主人战死沙场上　军犬复仇八年后

苏联卫国战争时期，谢·亚历山大罗维奇上校在某边防哨所任职期间，收养了一只名叫"文尔内"的大狼狗。这条狗的主人原是斯达罗斯基的军犬驯导员，不幸在一次与德国匪徒的激烈枪战中,中弹牺牲了。"文尔内"也两处负重伤。打扫战场时,人们在地上还发现了两个手指头,显然是当时狗扑向德国匪徒咬下来的。经过一阵治疗,"文尔内"的伤养好了,并已确定退役。上校收养了它。

八年后的一天,"文尔内"突然失踪不知去向,上校焦躁不安。两小时以后,值班军官报告:在市中心的街上,一条狼狗在凶猛地攻击一名德国人。上校立即乘车赶到现场。被咬的德国人刚刚死去,狗身上连中数弹,躺在一旁,但还活着。这时,上校看到了死者的右手,不禁惊愕:缺了两指!猛然间,他想起了八年前战友斯达罗斯基血洒战场的情景。

The Legend of Dog

The dog ranks the eleventh among the twelve animals in Chinese zodiac. It is associated with *Xu* in the Twelve Earthly Branches and the hours from 7:00 p.m. to 9:00 p.m. This is the time when people finish their daytime labor, close their doors and prepare to sleep. At this time the dog sleeps in front of the gate and guards the house. Therefore it is also named the "Dog of *Shu*".

Dogs were considered loyal since ancient times. Nowadays people love dogs even more, and think they come from "the planet of woof". Dog features countless folk artcrafts in the past and present, such as our beloved new-year pictures, clays and cloth crafts.

Legend 1: Brave and Loyal Dog Saves a Girl in Hurricane

Mr. and Mrs. Deke in the gull area of New Jersey, U.S. adopted a beautiful purebred New Finland dog and named it "Vella". The neighbor girl Antilia played with it every day after

十二生肖的传奇

school.

Yet on Feb.5, 1997, a hurricane struck the gull all of a sudden with the speed of 110 kilometers per hour. It blew Antilia into a snow pit only a few meters away from the coast. Vella found her and licked her awake with its warm tongue, and pulled Antilia outside of the pit with her holding its neck. Then the hurricane stroke again and threw her into the sea. Without hesitation, Vella ran into the sea and bit the clothes of Antilia

and swam to the shore. At last it took the girl home safe.

Not long after that Vella's story spread into the White House. On the celebration party of Christmas on Dec. 26, 1997, incumbent First Lady Hillary Clinton gave Vella a special badge to honor what it did.

Legend 2: Army Dog Avenges Its Owner Eight Years after His Death in the War

During the Soviet Union's Great Patriotic War against Nazi Germany, Colonel Shay Alexandrarovich brought up a big wolfhound named "Veroni" during his term of office in a frontier sentry. The previous owner of the wolfhound was a training officer of army dogs who was shot dead in a fierce battle with German gangsters. Veroni also received two severe wounds and lay beside its owner. When people cleaned the battlefield, they found two human fingers which were obviously bitten off by the wolfhound when it rushed onto the German gangster. After a period of medical treatment Veroni recovered and retired from the military service for sure. It was adopted by the colonel.

One day 8 year later, Veroni suddenly disappeared without a trace, which made the colonel restless. 2 hours later, the officer in duty reported that a wolfhound was fiercely rushing upon a German and was biting him on a downtown street. The colonel immediately took a car to the scene and saw the bitten German already dead. The dog was Veroni. It got several shots and was lying aside alive. At the moment, the colonel looked at the hand of the dead and could not help being shocked: there were two fingers missing in the hand! Suddenly he recalled the scene of his comrade-in-arms Staroski bathing in blood 8 years ago.

十二生肖传奇（中英文版）

猪的传奇

猪在十二生肖中居于最后一位,与十二地支中的"亥"相配。晚上九点至十一点,属"亥时"。这时候,夜深人静,常能听到猪拱槽的声音,故称"亥猪"。

在民俗文化中,人们普遍认为猪象征着财富。猪用鼻子拱地掘土求食,勤勤恳恳,老老实实,不奢望嗟来之食。

唐代科举考试,因"猪"与"朱"同音,"蹄"与"题"同音,所以赶考人的亲友们都赠送红烧猪蹄给他们吃,预祝赶考人"朱(猪)笔题(蹄)名"。

十二生肖的传奇

宋太祖赵匡胤曾亲自在宫中养了两头"神猪",供奉它们以祈求太平、避邪镇魔。在民间习俗中,猪的各个部位都寄寓吉祥的意义。猪头称为"神户",猪舌头叫"招财",猪耳朵则叫"顺风"。也有将猪头称为"利市",猪舌头称为"赚头"。这种寄寓吉祥的说法,最初根源于对猪的崇拜祭祀。

魏晋时期,流传着一个与猪共醉的故事。据说"竹林七贤"之一的阮咸请族人参加聚会,聚会上没有酒杯,而是随意拿起一种容器舀酒喝,甚至直接用手捧酒喝。在大家都喝得微醺之时,一位族人直接把头伸进酒缸里喝。其他人看到,也纷纷效仿,结果脸上、头发上沾满了酒,大家也都不在乎。这时候,阮咸家的猪走到酒缸前,将两只前蹄架在酒缸上,把头伸进去"呼噜呼噜"地大喝起来。阮咸和族人看到后更为兴奋,认为人猪共饮非常有趣,猪和人一样,理应自由快乐、没有束缚。

传奇一:波特兰市迷你猪 缉毒高手能力强

在美国俄勒岗州的波特兰市,有一头名叫"哈利"的越南迷你猪,已成为远近闻名的缉毒高手。警察卡什说:"别看年仅半岁的'哈利'是猪,但它的学习能力很强,比以聪明见称的警犬犹有过之。"猪的嗅觉灵敏,甚至能够嗅出埋在

十二生肖传奇（中英文版）

地下的毒品。

传奇二：几头猪崽真仗义　齐救落水农妇命

四川省有位农妇是养猪能手。她养的一头母猪和一群猪崽，个个膘肥体壮。

一天，她到屋后水塘提水喂猪，脚下一滑，跌入了水塘中。在生命垂危之际，她养的几头小猪崽隐约听到"救命"的呼救声，马上跑到塘边，一齐跳进水里，将农妇拱上了岸。

The Legend of Pig

The pig ranks the twelfth among the twelve animals in Chinese zodiac. It is associated with *Hai* in the Twelve Earthly Branches and the hours from 9:00 p.m. to 11:00 p.m. This is the time when the night is dark and people can hear the noise of the pig pushing the crib with its snout. Therefore it is also named the "Pig of *Hai*".

In folk culture, people think that the pig is a sign of

十二生肖的传奇

fortune. It digs the earth with the snout for food with honesty and veracity, never expecting a handout.

In the Tang Dynasty, people who took part in the imperial examinations were given braised pig hoof to eat to pray for a good grade. For the Chinese pronunciations for 猪(pig) and 朱(red) are both "*zhu*", 蹄(hoof) and 提(list) both "*ti*", eating "pig hoof" was a wish for their names written with "red" pen on the "list" of the top grades.

Zhao Kuangyi, Emperor Taizu of Song Dynasty, raised two "sacred pigs" by himself in his palace. He consecrated to them, to wish for peace and quench the evil spirits. In folk

traditions, all parts of the pig are given lucky names. The pig head is referred to as "godly house", the pig tongue "bringing fortune", the pig ear "smooth going". Other sayings are: "profits" for the pig head, "gaining" for the pig tongue. The lucky sayings originated in the worship of the pig.

In the Wei and Jin Dynasties there was a story about drinking wine together with a pig. Ruan Xian, one of the "Seven Sages of the Bamboo Grove", held a party within his clan. He invited his clansmen to drink wine, using no wine glass but any other container or even their hands. When they were all a little drunk, someone just stuck his head into the wine jar to drink. Others did the same, and nobody cared about their hair or faces that were covered with wine. At the moment, Ruan Xian's

pig came and also put its head into the jar. It put its hooves on the rim of the jar and gulped the wine. Ruan Xian and others thought it was very interesting to have a drink with the pig, for pig should be free and happy like human.

Legend 1: Mini Pig in Portland, Drug Enforcement Elite

In Portland City, Oregon State of the U.S., a famous mini Vietnam pig named "Harley" was recruited in a drug enforcement team with the police. Its "co-worker", Officer Cash said, "In spite of the fact that Harley is a pig, it has great learning ability, even better than some police dogs known to be smart." The pig enjoys a keen sense of sniffing, and it can detect the drugs buried underground.

Legend 2: Piglets with Loyal Hearts Saved Their Owner from Drowning

A peasant woman in Sichuan Province was good at raising pigs. She had a sow and a herd of piglets, all fat and strong.

One day she went to the pond behind the house to fetch water for the pigs, and slid into the pond by accident. When she

was about to drown, the piglets she raised heard her calls for help, and ran to the pond. They jumped into the water together and pulled her up from the pond.